Always remember to let Jesus be the center of your joy!

Bonita Williams

Dear Daughters

"REMEMBERING THE CENTER OF OUR JOY"

Dear Daughters

"Remembering the Center of Our Joy"

BONITA L. WILLIAMS

VISION INSPIRED PUBLICATIONS
ATLANTA, GEORGIA

DEDICATION

This book is dedicated to my mother, Mary Hood, whose warmth and support have shown me what true love is. THANKS, Mom, for all you've done for me.

ACKNOWLEDGMENTS

I am very grateful that God is not only a God of a second chance, but He is the God of many chances. God has lovingly guided me through the writing, editing and publishing process to produce a book that is meant to totally honor Him.

I also want to offer a word of thanks to the countless number of persons who have prayed for this book.

Additional thanks go out to the following people:

- My daughters Benecia and Breyuna, for always being in my corner.

- My granddaughter Amber, who keeps a smile on my face.

- My god–daughters Anthea, Franmicka and Stephanie, for their unconditional love and support.

- My editor Karen, for her invaluable service to this assignment.

- My sounding board Jacqueline, for lending me her ears.

PREFACE

Satan is on the warpath, seeking to destroy all that believe. We must declare our faith in God. We must determine in our hearts that for Christ we will live and for Christ we will die. Die to our self-centeredness, die to our wanting our own way, die to not doing God's will. It is time for us, the daughters of God, to take a stand. The letters contained in this volume address issues that we might face at one time or another.

I was given the blessed opportunity to share in rearing two beautiful daughters, Benecia and Breyuna. I watched them grow from a seed in my womb to truly wonderful God-fearing individuals. When God first gave me the inspiration to write *Dear Daughters* I thought the letters were for them. I started writing letters to my daughters when they were very young. I found that often the tone of my voice and the emotions in my heart hampered our communications. When I wrote a letter they were able to read it and digest the message without the interference of attitude. The message could then be digested and discussed on a different level. God helped me realize that *Dear Daughters* was to be a message to all His daughters, not just the two He lent to me.

The writing of these letters began May, 1997. God gave me the title of each letter to be written. I allowed doubt to convince me that I had misinterpreted God's direction in the matter. I wasn't a writer. He didn't plan for me to write. I put the idea on the back burner, but it kept coming to the surface. I told myself that it was too late, but God reminded me that He was in charge and that it is never too late. I asked for God's forgiveness of my slothfulness and doubts and then began to pray for guidance as I waited for His direction and message for His letters to be written. What you are reading are the letters inspired and directed by God. I take no credit for any of this. To God be the glory.

Bonita L. Williams

INTRODUCTION

Throughout life we will receive all kinds of advice. Bookstores are full of self-help books on how to build your finances; how to marry the right person; how to lose all those unwanted pounds. Society spends millions of dollars each year on self improvement books. The book with the most information on how we should live our lives is often the least read of all books. The book I am referring to is the Bible. In the Bible God speaks to us on every subject imaginable. There is nothing that the scriptures do not address. As you read, *Dear Daughters* "Remembering the Center of Our Joy", take time to read the scriptures that follow each letter. Choose one scripture that speaks to your heart and meditate on that scripture. Apply the word of God to your heart. Listen as GOD SPEAKS!

TO BE

Several years ago I read an article about compiling a "To Be List" to reflect on my relationship to God. Over the years I have begun some days of my life with a "to be" list rather than a "to do" list. "To do" list tend to make me focus more on my problems rather than on the problem solver. My "To Be" list allows me to place myself in God's will. I start with the letter A and end with the letter Z. Below is an example of one of my "To Be List."

A	Appreciative	N	Nice
B	Blessed	O	Obedient
C	Considerate	P	Patient
D	Devoted	Q	Quiet
E	Excited	R	Righteous
F	Faithful	S	Satisfied
G	Gentle	T	Truthful
H	Helpful	U	Unwavering
I	Interested	V	Victorious
J	Joyful	W	Willing
K	Kind	X	Exuberant
L	Loving	Y	Yielded
M	Mindful	Z	Zealous

Some of the words in the list I may change and some remain the same. The letters F. G, J, K, L, P, and S are frequently a part of the list. Those letters help focus on the fruit of the Spirit that dwells in all believers. In Galatians 5: 22-23, we are told that the fruit of the Spirit is love, joy, peace, patience, faith, goodness, kindness, gentleness, and self-control. I want God to stir up His spirit within me. Daily reflections on God and His wonderful faithfulness toward us can renew our spirit.

How to Use this Book:

God Speaks

At the end of each letter, you will find a section entitled **God Speaks**. The **God Speaks** section contains morsels from God's Word. Take time to think about God's goodness toward you. Ask the Holy Spirit to bring to your consciousness areas of concern of you might need to address.

Blessed Assurances

God's word contains messages and promises for each of us. At the end of each letter you will find a section entitled Blessed Assurances. Select a scripture from the God's Speaks section to reflect on each day. Write the scripture on the space provided. After reading and meditating on the scripture during the day take time to write down the assurance from our Father you received from the passage.

The Truth

At the end of the week you find a section entitled The Truth. Write out the truths that you gained during the week.

Thanksgivings

You will also find a space to write a prayer of thanksgiving to God for what He is doing in your life. Spending time with God each day will ensure that you will not become spiritually anemic.

Be blessed and rest in the comfort of the Lord

Bonita L. Williams

CONTENTS

Bonita L. Williams

WHOSE YOU ARE!!!
TRUE IDENTITY

Dear Daughters,

God uses many lessons to get us to where He wants us to be. He also places people in our lives to help us achieve the goals He has planned for us. One of the lessons I learned came to me many years ago. For years I thought I belonged to me. I went through life trying to satisfy myself. My life was totally centered on me. I was convinced that I knew what was best for me. My mother attempted to steer me in the right directions, but I wasn't always ready to listen. I didn't realize that my mother like many other women (daughters of God} had made a wonderful discovery and she was trying to share her wisdom with me. She knew who was truly in control. Mama's words of guidance often fell on my ears like a ton of bricks; they were just too much to bear. Her rules and advice just didn't fit in my plans. She had no earthly idea of what life was all about. I felt that she was trapped in the past and I was moving toward the future; our paths would never cross. I had no idea just how blind I was. It was not until I had a **personal experience** with God that I realized that the life I was using belonged to Christ. I had accepted Him as Savior at an early age, but I had not received Him as Lord of my life; I was under the assumption that I was still in control. I didn't know how to let Christ be the center of my life. The life I was using belonged to

Christ. The burdens I was trying to bear I did not have to bear any longer; the solution to every problem was suddenly at hand. Trying to take care of myself was a gigantic task; I just couldn't keep things running smoothly. Realizing that I did not have to worry about the issues of the world relieved me of unnecessary pressures. I was now free to truly enjoy the abundant life that Jesus had for me; a life full of peace and joy was mine. The moment trouble rises I can take it to the Lord in prayer and leave it there. I no longer have to carry thoughts of the past, concerns about today, or worries about tomorrow around with me. I finally understood the wisdom my mother was trying to share with me.

Years ago, God gave me an assurance scripture on which to cling when Satan was on the war path in my life. *"Fear thou not, for I am with thee, be not dismayed for I am thy God, I will strengthen thee, for I am with thee, yea I will uphold thee with my right hand of righteousness."* (Isaiah 41:10). If I choose to fear, it is because I choose to, not because I have to do so. True peace of mind belongs to me. I now know Whose I Am, **I belong to God.** I understand what my true identity is. So you see, Dear Daughters, you do not belong to yourself. You were bought with a price. The way you dress, your manner of conversation, your interaction with others is a reflection of your owner, **Jesus Christ.**

GOD SPEAKS...
WHOSE YOU ARE!!!
TRUE IDENTITY

JOHN 1:12

But as many as received him, to them gave the power to become the sons of God, even to them that believe on his name.

ROMANS 8:15

For ye have not received the spirit of bondage again to fear; but ye have received the Spirit of adoption, whereby we cry, Abba, Father.

EPHESIANS 2:19

Now therefore ye are no more strangers and foreigners, but fellow citizens with the saints, and of the household of God.

1PETER 1:3-5

Blessed be the God and Father of our Lord Jesus Christ, which according to his abundant mercy hath begotten us again unto a lively hope by the resurrection of Jesus Christ from the dead.

GENESIS 1:27

So God created man in his own image, in the image of God created he him; male and female created he them.

COLOSSIANS 3:12

Put on therefore, as the elect of God, holy and beloved, bowels of mercies, kindness, humbleness of mind, meekness, longsuffering.

JOHN 15:15

Henceforth I call you not servants; for the servant knoweth not what his lord doeth: but I have called you friends; for all things that I have heard of my Father I have made known unto you.

DEUTERONOMY 28:12

The LORD shall open unto thee his good treasure, the heaven to give the rain unto thy land in his season, and to bless all the work of thine hand: and thou shalt lend unto many nations, and thou shalt not borrow.

EPHESIANS 2:10

For we are his workmanship, created in Christ Jesus unto good works, which God hath before ordained that we should walk in them.

PHILIPPIANS 3:20

For our conversation is in heaven; from whence also we look for the Saviour, the Lord Jesus Christ.

1 CORINTHIANS 3:16

Know ye not that ye are the temple of God, and that the Spirit of God dwelleth in you?

ROMANS 8:17

And if children, then heirs; heirs of God, and joint-heirs with Christ; if so be that we suffer with him, that we may be also glorified together.

ROMANS 12:1-2

I beseech you therefore, brethren, by the mercies of God, that ye present your bodies a living sacrifice, holy, acceptable unto God, which is your reasonable service. And be not conformed to this world: but be ye transformed by the renewing of your mind, that ye may prove what is that good, and acceptable, and perfect, will of God.

PHILIPPIANS 4:13

I can do all things through Christ which strengtheneth me.

BLESSED ASSURANCES

Select a scripture from the *God Speaks* section to reflect on each day. Write the scripture in the space provided. After reading and meditating on the scripture during the day, take time to write down the assurance from our Father you received from the passage.

DAY1 _____

_____

_____

_____

DAY2 _____

_____

_____

_____

DAY3 _____

_____

_____

_____

DAY4 _____

_____

_____

DAY5_____

_____

_____

_____

DAY6_____

_____

_____

_____

DAY7_____

_____

_____

_____

THE TRUTH

Write out the truths that you gained during the week.

THANKSGIVINGS

Write a prayer of thanksgiving to God for what He is
doing in your life.

TIME WELL SPENT
Waiting on God

Dear Daughters,

What direction do I take? Where do I go from here? Who do I turn to? What am I to do? Questions, questions, and then more questions. What is the answer? JESUS!!! Jesus is the answer to all questions. I have heard that statement over and over from the time I was a little girl. "Jesus Loves Me" was one of the first songs I learned the words to, but as I grew older and experienced more circumstances I began to question how Christ could possibly love me. I made too many mistakes. I took two steps forward and it seemed I took ten steps backwards. Every time I thought I had things together the glue would not stick. I didn't know how to weather the storms of life. I thought, like many people, that once you came to Christ it would be smooth sailing. My thought was that I could just sit back and enjoy the ride. That was partially true. We are to sit back and let Jesus do the driving. But the ride is not always promised to be a smooth one. There are curves and bumps on the road of life. There are stormy seas, and valley experiences. We will encounter dangerous toils and snares. Just as the song says, God's grace has brought us safe thus far and His grace will lead us on. God's grace is sufficient for every situation. There's not a problem that God does not have answer for. Just wait on the Lord. Place your

trust in Him and He will direct your path. True waiting is something that most people find difficult to do. They want things right away. The scripture says "They that wait on the Lord shall renew their strength." (Isaiah 40:31).

As I have tried to apply this scripture to my life, I realize that I need to understand a couple of things. First of all the waiting part is not as easy as just making a statement. Human nature causes us to want to do something. We don't like waiting. We want something to happen instantaneously. A prayer prayed at 12:32 a.m. is expected to be answered by 12:37 a.m. at the latest. God has the power to answer our prayers right away if that is His will. But not all prayer requests are answered immediately in God's Word we find numerous examples of how people had to wait. David was promised to be king but he didn't become king until 20 years after the promise. God promised that Abraham would father a child but the promise did not come true for 15 years. The woman with the issue of blood prayed for 13 years before her prayer was answered. What we can learn from these individuals is that the time spent waiting on God is worth the wait. God knows the best timing for our lives. He will not always come when we think He should, but we have a guarantee that He will meet all of our needs right on time. The time spent waiting on the God is indeed time well spent.

GOD SPEAKS...
TIME WELL SPENT
(WAITING ON GOD)

PSALM 27:14

Wait on the LORD: be of good courage, and he shall strengthen thine heart: wait, I say, on the LORD.

ISAISH 40:31

But they that wait upon the LORD shall renew their strength; they shall mount up with wings as eagles; they shall run, and not be weary; and they shall walk, and not faint.

HABAKKUK 2:3

For the vision is yet for an appointed time, but at the end it shall speak, and not lie: though it tarry, wait for it; because it will surely come, it will not tarry.

1 CORINTHIANS 2:9

But as it is written, Eye hath not seen, nor ear heard, neither have entered into the heart of man, the things which God hath prepared for them that love him.

PSALM 25:4-5

Show me Your ways, O Lord; teach me Your paths. Lead me in Your truth and teach me: for You are the God of my salvation; on You do I wait all day.

PSALM 31:24

Be of good courage and He shall strengthen your heart, all you who wait for the Lord.

PSALM 33:20, 22

Our soul waits for the Lord: He is our help and our shield. Let Your mercy, O Lord, be upon us, as we wait for You.

PSALM 37:7, 9

Rest in the Lord, and wait patiently for Him... Those that wait upon the Lord, they shall inherit the earth.

PSALM 37:34

Wait on the Lord and keep His way, and He shall exalt thee to inherit the land.

PSALM 40:1

I waited patiently for the Lord; and He inclined to me and heard my cry.

PSALM 59:9

I will wait for You, oh You my strength, for God is my defense.

PSALM 62:5-6

My soul, wait silently for God alone; my hope is from Him. He only is my rock and my salvation.

ISAIAH 26:8-9

Yes, in the way of Your judgements, O Lord, have we waited for You. The desire of our souls is for Your name. With my soul I have desired You in the night, Yes, by my spirit within me I will seek You early.

BLESSED ASSURANCES

Select a scripture from the *God Speaks* section to reflect on each day. Write the scripture in the space provided. After reading and meditating on the scripture during the day, take time to write down the assurance from our Father you received from the passage.

DAY1_____

_____

_____

_____

DAY2_____

_____

_____

_____

DAY3_____

_____

_____

_____

DAY4_____

_____

_____

_____

DAY5_____

_____

_____

_____

DAY6_____

_____

_____

_____

DAY7_____

_____

_____

_____

THE TRUTH

Write out the truths that you gained during the week.

THANKSGIVINGS

Write a prayer of thanksgiving to God for what He is

doing in your life.

FIRST THINGS FIRST
SEEK GOD FIRST

Dear Daughters,

What a pity it is that we waste so much time trying to learn how to live. By the time many people discover life's true meaning it's time to die. Maturity for many is accompanied by wisdom. But one doesn't have to wait until the hair on the head is white and the steps are feeble to gain wisdom (James 1:5). If we want to know which direction to go, we just have to ask. God has promised to direct our paths (Proverbs 3:6). We must be careful though not to think more highly of ourselves than we ought (Romans 12:3). When the blessings flow, we must acknowledge their origin. We are not to go on our thoughts but the thoughts of God. God tells us to seek His kingdom first and all things we need will be added (Matthew 6:33). We are not to make decisions and then ask God what He thinks about them. We are to seek His guidance first before we make any decisions. "What college should I attend?" What career should I choose?" "What should I do with my life?" "Who will be my mate?" "Should I purchase this…?" "Is this in your will for me to…?" We must strive to use the guide God has given to us to gain knowledge. God wants us to seek Him first before we make any decision because He already knows what's best for us. As stated earlier, God has all the answers to all our

questions. Our part is to seek His direction. Our plans should reflect the will of God. Proverbs 4:7 tells us that "Wisdom is the principal thing; therefore get wisdom: and with all thy getting get understanding."

Spending time in prayer and meditation will allow us to keep our priorities straight. It will be easier for us to know just what to do in most cases. Remember in James1:5 we find a promise that God will freely give us wisdom in a generous portion. Daily say as David did that God's Word is indeed "a lamp unto our feet and a light unto our path." Seek God first and He will handle the rest.

GOD SPEAKS...
FIRST THINGS FIRST
(SEEK GOD FIRST)

DEUTERONOMY 13:4

Ye shall walk after the LORD your God, and fear him, and keep his commandments, and obey his voice, and ye shall serve him, and cleave unto him.

PSALM 23:3

He restoreth my soul: he leadeth me in the paths of righteousness for his name's sake.

PSALM 32:8

I will instruct thee and teach thee in the way which thou shalt go: I will guide thee with mine eye.

PSALM 37:23-24

The steps of a good man are ordered by the LORD: and he delighteth in his way. Though he fall, he shall not be utterly cast down: for the LORD upholdeth him with his hand.

PSALM 48:14

For this God is our God for ever and ever: he will be our guide even unto death.

PSALM 37:4-7

Delight thyself also in the LORD: and he shall give thee the desires of thine heart. Commit thy way unto the LORD; trust also in him; and he shall bring it to pass. And he shall bring forth thy righteousness as the light, and thy judgment as the noonday. Rest in the LORD, and wait patiently for him: fret not thyself because of him who prospereth in his way, because of the man who bringeth wicked devices to pass.

PROVERBS 16:9

A man's heart deviseth his way: but the LORD directeth his steps.

PROVERBS 1:33

But whoso hearkeneth unto me shall dwell safely, and shall be quiet from fear of evil.

PROVERBS 3:5, 6

Trust in the LORD with all thine heart; and lean not unto thine own understanding. In all thy ways acknowledge him, and he shall direct thy paths.

JEREMIAH 29:11

For I know the thoughts that I think toward you, saith the LORD, thoughts of peace, and not of evil, to give you an expected end.

PSALM 119:105

Thy word is a lamp unto my feet, and a light unto my path.

ISAIAH 48:17

Thus saith the LORD, thy Redeemer, the Holy One of Israel; I am the LORD thy God which teacheth thee to profit, which leadeth thee by the way that thou shouldest go.

ISAIAH 58:11

And the LORD shall guide thee continually, and satisfy thy soul in drought, and make fat thy bones: and thou shalt be like a watered garden, and like a spring of water, whose waters fail not.

MATTHEW 6:33

But seek ye first the kingdom of God, and his righteousness; and all these things shall be added unto you.

ROMANS 12:3

For I say, through the grace given unto me, to every man that is among you, not to think of himself more highly than he ought to think; but to think soberly, according as God hath dealt to every man the measure of faith.

BLESSED ASSURANCES

Select a scripture from the *God Speaks* section to reflect on each day. Write the scripture in the space provided. After reading and meditating on the scripture during the day, take time to write down the assurance from our Father you received from the passage.

DAY1_____

_____

_____

_____

_____

_____

DAY2_____

_____

_____

_____

_____

DAY3____   _____

_____

_____

_____

DAY4_____

_____

_____

_____

DAY5_____

_____

_____

_____

DAY6_____

_____

_____

_____

DAY7_____

_____

_____

_____

THE TRUTH

Write out the truths that you gained during the week.

THANKSGIVINGS
Write a prayer of thanksgiving to God for what He is

doing in your life. HELPING HANDS

HELPING HANDS
HOLY SPIRIT

Dear Daughters,

What a blessing it is to realize that we are not alone in this world. God has placed in each of our lives someone to be our companion. When Christ explained to His disciples that He was leaving earth to return to heaven, He promised that He would not leave them comfortless. Jesus told them they would receive the Holy Spirit. Not only was that a promise for the earlier disciples, it applies to Christ's disciples today.

We have the gift of the Holy Spirit. Once we accepted Christ as Lord and Savior, the Holy Spirit took up residence in our lives. I didn't understand this when I accepted Christ as Savior. I believed that I was saved and would go to heaven when I died, but I didn't know how to give Jesus the proper place as Lord of my life. I didn't know what it meant to totally surrender my will. I spent years waiting for the Holy Spirit to come. While waiting I continued to try to handle things on my own. I worried and fretted over almost everything. I went through the motions, but I still knew something was wrong. I didn't have that peace that surpasses all understanding (Philippians 4:7).

Through the gentle prompting of the Holy Spirit I came to realize that all I had to do was let go. Just LET GO!!! Let go of what? I had to completely give my life to Christ. I had to become a lump of clay on the potter's wheel. I had to purpose in my heart that Christ was all and all.

I don't want to make light of this issue. When you come to the point of total surrender Satan is standing there at the crossroads. He tries to lie to you and convince you that you've made a mistake. He gets in your family, your loved ones and even you. He tries to cause all kinds of confusion. He tells you that you must hold on to your will. It's yours. You need it. Not so..."Not our will, but Thy will be done," is the prayer Christ taught us to pray.

In order to enjoy the true benefits of having the Holy Spirit as part of our lives we must be willing to totally surrender our lives to Christ. In our cars we use cruise control when we want the car to take over navigation. We must learn to put our lives in Holy Spirit control and let Christ take over.

The helping hand of the Holy Spirit becomes ours the moment we accept Christ as Lord and Savior. Accept the help of the Comforter and enjoy the ride. Allow the Holy Spirit to do His job in your life.

GOD SPEAKS...
HELPING HANDS
(THE HOLY SPIRIT)

JOHN 14:16-17

And I will pray the Father, and he shall give you another Comforter, that he may abide with you for ever; Even the Spirit of truth; whom the world cannot receive, because it seeth him not, neither knoweth him: but ye know him; for he dwelleth with you, and shall be in you.

PHILIPPIANS 1:6

Being confident of this very thing, that he which hath begun a good work in you will perform it until the day of Jesus Christ:

JOHN 14:26

But the Comforter, which is the Holy Ghost, whom the Father will send in my name, he shall teach you all things, and bring all things to your remembrance, whatsoever I have said unto you.

JOHN 16:13-14

Howbeit when he, the Spirit of truth, is come, he will guide you into all truth: for he shall not speak of himself; but whatsoever he shall hear, that shall he speak: and he will shew you things to come. He shall glorify me: for he shall receive of mine, and shall shew it unto you.

1 Corinthians 6:19

What? know ye not that your body is the temple of the Holy Ghost which is in you, which ye have of God, and ye are not your own?

Romans 5:5

[5]And hope maketh not ashamed; because the love of God is shed abroad in our hearts by the Holy Ghost which is given unto us.

John 14:16-17

And I will pray the Father, and he shall give you another Comforter, that he may abide with you forever. Even the Spirit of truth; whom the world cannot receive, because it seeth him not, neither knoweth him: but ye know him; for he dwelleth with you, and shall be in you.

John 16:7-8, 13

Nevertheless I tell you the truth; it is expedient for you that I go away: for if I go not away, the Comforter will not come unto you; but if I depart, I will send him unto you. And when he is come, he will reprove the world of sin, and of righteousness, and of judgment. Howbeit when he, the Spirit of truth, is come, he will guide you into all truth: for he shall not speak of himself; but whatsoever he shall hear, that shall he speak: and he will shew you things to come.

ROMANS 8:5-6

For they that are after the flesh do mind the things of the flesh; but they that are after the Spirit the things of the Spirit. or to be carnally minded is death; but to be spiritually minded is life and peace.

ROMANS 8:14

For as many as are led by the Spirit of God, they are the sons of God.

ROMANS 8:26-27

Likewise the Spirit also helpeth our infirmities: for we know not what we should pray for as we ought: but the Spirit itself maketh intercession for us with groanings which cannot be uttered. And he that searcheth the hearts knoweth what is the mind of the Spirit, because he maketh intercession for the saints according to the will of God.

EPHESIANS 3:16

That he would grant you, according to the riches of his glory, to be strengthened with might by his Spirit in the inner man;

JOHN 16:12-13

I have yet many things to say unto you, but ye cannot bear them now. Howbeit when he, the Spirit of truth, is come, he will guide you into all truth: for he shall not speak of himself; but whatsoever he shall hear, that shall he speak: and he will shew you things to come.

ROMANS 8:26

Likewise the Spirit also helpeth our infirmities: for we know not what we should pray for as we ought: but the Spirit itself maketh intercession for us with groanings which cannot be utteredmaketh intercession for us with groanings which cannot be uttered.

1 CORINTHIANS 2:10-11

But God hath revealed them unto us by his Spirit: for the Spirit searcheth all things, yea, the deep things of God. For what man knoweth the things of a man, save the spirit of man which is in him? even so the things of God knoweth no man, but the Spirit of God.

BLESSED ASSURANCES

Select a scripture from the *God Speaks* section to reflect on each day. Write the scripture in the space provided. After reading and meditating on the scripture during the day, take time to write down the assurance from our Father you received from the passage.

DAY1_____

_____

_____

_____

DAY2_____

_____

_____

_____

DAY3_____

_____

_____

_____

DAY4_____

_____

_____

_____

DAY5 _____

_____

_____

_____

DAY6 _____

_____

_____

_____

DAY7 _____

_____

_____

_____

THE TRUTH
Write out the truths that you gained during the week.

THANKSGIVINGS
Write a prayer of thanksgiving to God for what He is doing in your life.

THROUGH THE EYES OF THE FATHER
GOD'S CREATION

Dear Daughters,

Life has a way of distorting our vision. We often see only part of the picture. While being caught up with the troubles of this world we fail to see its beauty. We fail to see the beauty of a new day if we focus on the problems that seem to block our paths. We fail to see the beauty of a true friendship or the beauty of a caring family member, friend, or co-worker when we focus on what we don't have instead of seeing the blessings we have been given. We fail to see what a wonderful creation we are when we measure ourselves against man's standards.

We must learn to see ourselves through the eyes of the Father. Our heavenly Father has shaped us after His own image. We are His. God is the designer. We are not to see ourselves as too this or too that. We are to see ourselves as picture images created by God.

Impossible you may say. "I'm not the perfect size."

"My feet are…"

My lips…"

"My hair…"

"I don't…"

"I can't…:

"I haven't…"

These sentences can be completed by many poor images of us.

The above-mentioned items deal solely with man's measure of us. We should move from viewing ourselves as others see us to what God sees. We must look for the beauty in our life. Through the Father's eyes we see the beauty of our soul. We come to realize that we are precious treasures in earthen vessels (2 Corinthians 4:7).

Do you really think Christ would have given His life if we were not of value to Him?

Stop seeing yourself as man sees you. Focus on the beauty that God created.

GOD SPEAKS...
THROUGH THE EYES OF THE FATHER
(GOD'S CREATION)

1 SAMUEL 16:7

But the LORD said unto Samuel, Look not on his countenance, or on the height of his stature; because I have refused him: for the LORD seeth not as man seeth; for man looketh on the outward appearance, but the LORD looketh on the heart.

PSALM 139:14-15

I will praise thee; for I am fearfully and wonderfully made: marvelous are thy works; and that my soul knoweth right well. My substance was not hid from thee, when I was made in secret, and curiously wrought in the lowest parts of the earth.

PROVERB 31:30

Favour is deceitful, and beauty is vain: but a woman that feareth the LORD, she shall be praised.

1 PETER 3:3-4

Whose adorning let it not be that outward adorning of plaiting the hair, and of wearing of gold, or of putting on of apparel. But let it be the hidden man of the heart, in that which is not corruptible, even the ornament of a meek and quiet spirit, which is in the sight of God of great price.

2 CORINTHIANS 10-7

Do ye look on things after the outward appearance? if any man trust to himself that he is Christ's, let him of himself think this again, that, as he is Christ's, even so are we Christ's.

PSALM 100:3

Know ye that the LORD he is God: it is he that hath made us, and not we ourselves; we are his people, and the sheep of his pasture.

EPHESIANS 2:10

For we are his workmanship, created in Christ Jesus unto good works, which God hath before ordained that we should walk in them.

ISAIAH 43:1

But now thus saith the LORD that created thee, O Jacob, and he that formed thee, O Israel, Fear not: for I have redeemed thee, I have called thee by thy name; thou art mine.

PSALM 149:4

For the LORD taketh pleasure in his people: he will beautify the meek with salvation.

PSALM 139:13-16 (MSG)

Oh yes, you shaped me first inside, then out; you formed me in my mother's womb. I thank you, High God—you're breathtaking! Body and soul, I am marvelously made! I worship in adoration—what a creation!   You know me inside and out, you know every bone in my body; You know exactly how I was made, bit by bit, how I was sculpted from nothing into something.   Like an open book, you watched me grow from conception to birth; all the stages of my life were spread out before you. The days of my life all prepared before I'd even lived one day.

2 CORINTHIANS 10:7

Do ye look on things after the outward appearance? if any man trust to himself that he is Christ's, let him of himself think this again, that, as he is Christ's, even so are we Christ's

JEREMIAH 31:3

The LORD hath appeared of old unto me, saying, Yea, I have loved thee with an everlasting love: therefore with loving kindness have I drawn thee.

1 PETER 3:3-4

Whose adorning let it not be that outward adorning of plaiting the hair, and of wearing of gold, or of putting on of apparel. But let it be the hidden man of the heart, in that which is not corruptible, even the ornament of a meek and quiet spirit, which is in the sight of God of great price.

PROVERBS 31:30

Favour is deceitful, and beauty is vain: but a woman that feareth the LORD, she shall be praised.

BLESSED ASSURANCES

Select a scripture from the *God Speaks* section to reflect on each day. Write the scripture in the space provided. After reading and meditating on the scripture during the day, take time to write down the assurance from our Father you received from the passage.

DAY1_____

_____

_____

_____

DAY2_____

_____

_____

_____

DAY3_____

_____

_____

_____

DAY4_____

_____

_____

_____

DAY5_____

_____

_____

_____

DAY6_____

_____

_____

_____

DAY7_____

_____

_____

_____

THE TRUTH

Write out the truths that you gained during the week.

THANKSGIVINGS

Write a prayer of thanksgiving to God for what He is doing in your life.

WINNING EDGE
VICTORY WITH JESUS

Dear Daughters,

If the truth were known many people have discovered that they missed many years of true happiness looking in the wrong places. "Oh what peace we often forfeit. Oh what needless pains we bear all because we do not carry everything to God in prayer." These words to a familiar hymn explain the plight of many people. Joy, unspeakable joy is available to every believer. One doesn't have to wait until the right moment to enjoy life. We don't have to search any further than our prayers and our relationship with God. God has so many wonderful things waiting for us just for the asking. Jesus told us "He came that we might have life and have it more abundantly" (John 10:10). Now, just what does that mean? Does it mean that I will have no more troubles? Or does it mean that I will not experience any grief or pain? Will everything be smooth sailing?

No, that's not what abundant life means. The truth is there will be trials and tribulations. There might even be some pain and sorrow. The wonderful thing is that with each situation you are given the blessed assurance that you will come out a winner. You have a guaranteed promise that God will never leave you alone. In Isaiah 43:2 God's Word tells us that He will be with us when we go through our rainy and fiery experiences. So no matter what you face, God is on your side. Victory is already ours. Jesus agreed to leave Heaven and live on Earth to go through the same things we go through. He was hungry, tempted, lonely, and rejected, and faced many of the other emotions that we encounter. He suffered in order for us to understand the depth of God's love for us. Mankind's sin separates us from God. Jesus endured the agony of Calvary just so that we could be put in right relationship with God. Once we accepted Christ as Savior we entered the winner's circle. True victory is ours. We joined the family of God. We can experience the abundance of joy, love, and peace God has for us. No matter what situations we find ourselves in, we can rejoice and remember that we always have the winning edge. Regardless of how things seem we can place our trust in God with the full knowledge that we are winners. Rejoice and reflect on all the things God has already done and all the things He promises to do for those that lean and depend on Him. When we think about these things we realize we truly have the winning edge.

GOD SPEAKS...
WINNING EDGE
(VICTORY WITH JESUS)

DEUTERONOMY 31:8

And the LORD, he it is that doth go before thee; he will be with thee, he will not fail thee, neither forsake thee: fear not, neither be dismayed.

NAHUM 1:7

The LORD is good, a strong hold in the day of trouble; and he knoweth them that trust in him.

PSALM 9:10

And they that know thy name will put their trust in thee: for thou, LORD, hast not forsaken them that seek thee.

JOSHUA 1:8

This book of the law shall not depart out of thy mouth; but thou shalt meditate therein day and night, that thou mayest observe to do according to all that is written therein: for then thou shalt make thy way prosperous, and then thou shalt have good success.

2 CORINTHIANS 3:5 (NLT)

It is not that we think we are qualified to do anything on our own. Our qualification comes from God.

DEUTERONOMY 28:12-13 (NKJV)

The LORD will open to you His good treasure, the heavens, to give the rain to your land in its season, and to bless all the work of your hand. You shall lend to many nations, but you shall not borrow. And the LORD will make you the head and not the tail; you shall be above only, and not be beneath, if you heed the commandments of the LORD your God, which I command you today, and are careful to observe them.

1 SAMUEL 18:14 (NIV)

In everything he did he had great success, because the LORD was with him.

1 CORINTHIANS 15:57

But thanks be to God, which giveth us the victory through our Lord Jesus Christ.

PHILIPPIANS 4:13

I can do all things through Christ which strengtheneth me.

EPHESIANS 1:3-8

Blessed be the God and Father of our Lord Jesus Christ, who hath blessed us with all spiritual blessings in heavenly places in Christ: According as he hath chosen us in him before the foundation of the world, that we should be holy and without blame before him in love: Having predestinated us unto the adoption of children by Jesus Christ to himself, according to the good pleasure of his will, To the praise of the glory of his grace, wherein he hath made us accepted in the beloved. In whom we have redemption through his blood, the forgiveness of sins, according to the riches of his grace. Wherein he hath abounded toward us in all wisdom and prudence.

COLOSSIANS 1:13-14

³Who hath delivered us from the power of darkness, and hath translated us into the kingdom of his dear Son. In whom we have redemption through his blood, even the forgiveness of sins.

COLOSSIANS 2:9-10

For in him dwelleth all the fulness of the Godhead bodily. And ye are complete in him, which is the head of all principality and power.

HEBREWS 4:14-16

Seeing then that we have a great high priest that is passed into the heavens, Jesus the Son of God; let us hold fast our profession. For we have not an high priest which cannot be touched with the feeling of our infirmities; but was in all points tempted like as we are, yet without sin. Let us therefore come boldly unto the throne of grace that we may obtain mercy, and find grace to help in time of need.

ROMANS 8:31-39

What shall we then say to these things? If God be for us, who can be against us? He that spared not his own Son, but delivered him up for us all, how shall he not with him

also freely give us all things? Who shall lay any thing to the charge of God's elect? It is God that justifieth. Who is he that condemneth? It is Christ that died, yea rather, that is risen again, who is even at the right hand of God, who also maketh intercession for us. Who shall separate us from the love of Christ? shall tribulation, or distress, or persecution, or famine, or nakedness, or peril, or sword? As it is written, For thy sake we are killed all the day long; we are accounted as sheep for the slaughter. Nay, in all these things we are more than conquerors through him that loved us. For I am persuaded, that neither death, nor life, nor angels, nor principalities, nor powers, nor things present, nor things to come, Nor height, nor depth, nor any other creature, shall be able to separate us from the love of God, which is in Christ Jesus our Lord.

BLESSED ASSURANCES

Select a scripture from the *God Speaks* section to reflect on each day. Write the scripture in the space provided. After reading and meditating on the scripture during the day, take time to write down the assurance from our Father you received from the passage.

DAY1_____

_____

_____

_____

DAY2_____

_____

_____

_____

DAY3_____

_____

_____

_____

DAY4_____

_____

_____

_____

DAY5_____

_____

_____

_____

DAY6_____

_____

_____

_____

DAY7_____

_____

_____

_____

THE TRUTH

Write out the truths that you gained during the week.

THANKSGIVINGS

Write a prayer of thanksgiving to God for what He is
doing in your life.

SEARCH NO MORE
JESUS IS OUR FRIEND

Dear Daughters,

One of my favorite songs begins by stating that we have a friend in Jesus. The song continues on by saying that He will bear all our sins and grief. According to the song all we have to do is take it to Him in prayer. Take it to the Lord in prayer. Just what is it? What should we take to God in prayer? Why should I accept the friendship of Jesus? The world is full of uncertainties. Prices are constantly rising, corporations are downsizing, and crime is on the rampage. Nothing is sure. We enter human relationships not sure how things are going to work out. We dare not make a commitment to anyone for fear of disappointment. Where do we turn? Who can we trust? Where do we go to find true friendship? Who is there that will not let us down? We search for answers to our questions in all the wrong places- friends, family, New Age thinkers. Let me suggest an answer to all of your questions. Turn to Jesus and your quest for knowledge will be eased. Jesus stated that He is "the way, the truth, and the life" (John 14:6).

Turn to Jesus and your searching will be over. Turn to Jesus; He is your best friend. Jesus bore the cross because of a love for you. If you are looking for the answer to all that ails you, turn to Jesus. He can supply all the answers to the

questions you have. Jesus is the one that sticks closer than a brother. Looking for a friend? Looking for someone to share the load? Search no more! Turn to Jesus! I have found that the "it" mentioned in the song refers to whatever worries, concerns or cares we have. We should give Jesus everything. Take everything to the Lord and leave it with Him. Let go of the struggle. Accept the fact that the battle is not yours, it's the Lord's. He has already paid the price on Calvary. John 15:13 tells us that "Greater love has no one than this, that he lay down his life for his friends." Jesus gave His life for us. Don't allow fear to grip your life. Daily place your cares at the feet of Jesus and leave them there. There is no need to search any further than Jesus. **Your friend Jesus will always be there for you.**

GOD SPEAKS...
SEARCH NO MORE
(JESUS IS OUR FRIEND)

JOHN 14:23

Jesus answered and said unto him, If a man love me, he will keep my words: and my Father will love him, and we will come unto him, and make our abode with him.

JOHN 15:4-7

Abide in me, and I in you. As the branch cannot bear fruit of itself, except it abide in the vine; no more can ye, except ye abide in me. I am the vine, ye are the branches: He that abideth in me, and I in him, the same bringeth forth much fruit: for without me ye can do nothing. If a man abide not in me, he is cast forth as a branch, and is withered; and men gather them, and cast them into the fire, and they are burned. If ye abide in me, and my words abide in you, ye shall ask what ye will, and it shall be done unto you.

JOHN 15:13-15

Greater love hath no man than this, that a man lay down his life for his friends. Ye are my friends, if ye do whatsoever I command you. Henceforth I call you not servants; for the servant knoweth not what his lord doeth: but I have called you friends; for all things that I have heard of my Father I have made known unto you.

REVELATION 3:20

Behold, I stand at the door, and knock: if any man hear my voice, and open the door, I will come in to him, and will sup with him, and he with me.

1 CORINTHIANS 1:9

God is faithful, by whom ye were called unto the fellowship of his Son Jesus Christ our Lord.

1 JOHN 1:3

That which we have seen and heard declare we unto you, that ye also may have fellowship with us: and truly our fellowship is with the Father, and with his Son Jesus Christ.

JOHN 14:18

I will not leave you comfortless: I will come to you.

GALATIANS 3:26

For ye are all the children of God by faith in Christ Jesus.

JOHN 1:12

But as many as received him, to them gave he power to become the sons of God, even to them that believe on his name.

BLESSED ASSURANCES

Select a scripture from the *God Speaks* section to reflect on each day. Write the scripture in the space provided. After reading and meditating on the scripture during the day, take time to write down the assurance from our Father you received from the passage.

DAY1 _____

_____

_____

_____

DAY2 _____

_____

_____

_____

DAY3 _____

_____

_____

_____

DAY4 _____

_____

_____

_____

DAY5_____

_____

_____

_____

DAY6_____

_____

_____

_____

DAY7_____

_____

_____

_____

THE TRUTH
Write out the truths that you gained during the week.

THANKSGIVINGS
Write a prayer of thanksgiving to God for what He is
doing in your life.

HONESTY
TRUTH

Dear Daughters,

We often forfeit peace and bear unnecessary pains. We do so all because we choose not to take **everything** to God in prayer. We want to handle things on our own.

Believe it or not some people think they can pull something over on God. "If I don't pray, if I stop having my mediation time; if I just keep to myself God will never know." Sounds ridiculous doesn't it, but that is just what happens when we slip up or backslide. Satan would have us believe that God no longer wants to hear from us when we sin. Oh what a great deceiver Satan is. He wants us to believe that God separates Himself from us when we falter. This is the farthest thing from the truth. 1 John 1:9 states that "if we confess our sins God is faithful to forgive and cleanse us from all unrighteousness."

God's Word also tells us that nothing can separate us from God's love. The truth of the matter is Satan wants us to feel alienated, lonely, lost, embarrassed, and frustrated, and the list goes on and on. God is a loving Father who gave His only begotten Son to save us. What a price to pay. Don't believe the lies of the devil. Go to God in prayer. Honestly tell Him what's in your heart. God wants to have an intimate relationship with you. He already knows all there is to

know about you. He is our creator. When we sincerely and truthfully confess our sins to God, He promises to cleanse us. He doesn't want us to be afraid of Him. He wants us to have fear of Him, which means He wants us to show reverence Him. We are to acknowledge who He is and give Him the proper place in our lives. As creator He deserves our profound respect and awe. We don't have to spend our days in dread and despair. God truly loves us. He definitely does not like some of the choices we make, but that still doesn't change the love He has for us. The Bible states that we will reap what we sow. The reaping time is not an indication that God has stopped loving us. Don't try to pull the wool over His eyes. Remember God knows and sees all. Be honest with Him and experience His loving cleansing power.

GOD SPEAKS...
HONESTY
(TRUTH)

NAHUM 1:7

The LORD is good, a strong hold in the day of trouble; and he knoweth them that trust in him.

ISAIAH 43:2

When thou passest through the waters, I will be with thee; and through the rivers, they shall not overflow thee: when thou walkest through the fire, thou shalt not be burned; neither shall the flame kindle upon thee.

ISAIAH 1:18

Come now, and let us reason together, saith the LORD: though your sins be as scarlet, they shall be as white as snow; though they be red like crimson, they shall be as wool.

JEREMIAH 33:8

And I will cleanse them from all their iniquity, whereby they have sinned against me; and I will pardon all their iniquities, whereby they have sinned, and whereby they have transgressed against me.

JOHN 14:1

Let not your heart be troubled: ye believe in God, believe also in me.

1 CORINTHIANS 1:3-4

Grace be unto you, and peace, from God our Father, and from the Lord Jesus Christ. I thank my God always on your behalf, for the grace of God which is given you by Jesus Christ.

COLOSSIANS 3:9-10

Lie not one to another, seeing that ye have put off the old man with his deeds. And have put on the new man, which is renewed in knowledge after the image of him that created him.

PROVERBS 11:1

A false balance is abomination to the LORD: but a just weight is his delight

PHILIPPIANS 4:8-9

Finally, brethren, whatsoever things are true, whatsoever things are honest, whatsoever things are just, whatsoever things are pure, whatsoever things are lovely, whatsoever things are of good report; if there be any virtue, and if there be any praise, think on these things. Those things, which ye have both learned, and received, and heard, and seen in me, do: and the God of peace shall be with you.

PROVERBS 10:9

He that walketh uprightly walketh surely: but he that perverteth his ways shall be known.

1 CHRONICLES 29:17

I know also, my God, that thou triest the heart, and hast

pleasure in uprightness. As for me, in the uprightness of mine heart I have willingly offered all these things: and now have I seen with joy thy people, which are present here, to offer willingly unto thee.

LUKE 8:15 (NASB)

But the seed in the good soil, these are the ones who have heard the word in an honest and good heart, and hold it fast, and bear fruit with perseverance.

ROMANS 9:1 (NASB)

I say the truth in Christ, I lie not, my conscience testifies with me in the Holy Spirit.

PSALM 119: 142 (NLT)

Your justice is eternal, and Your instructions are perfectly true.

BLESSED ASSURANCES

Select a scripture from the *God Speaks* section to reflect on each day. Write the scripture in the space provided. After reading and meditating on the scripture during the day, take time to write down the assurance from our Father you received from the passage.

DAY1_____

_____

_____

_____

DAY2_____

_____

_____

_____

DAY3_____

_____

_____

_____

DAY4_____

_____

_____

_____

DAY5_____

_____

_____

_____

DAY6_____

_____

_____

_____

DAY7_____

_____

_____

_____

THE TRUTH

Write out the truths that you gained during the week.

THANKSGIVINGS

Write a prayer of thanksgiving to God for what He is doing in your life.

W.O.W
WINNING OVER WILL

Dear Daughters,

"Thy will be done," is part of the model prayer taught to the disciples by Christ when they asked Him to teach them how to pray (Matthew 6:9-13). The acceptance of Christ as our personal Savior is a wonderful experience. We have the blessed assurance that Jesus shed His blood for us and a seat in Heaven is waiting for us upon our arrival. We are given the joy that comes with salvation. But does it go further than that? Just what does accepting Christ involve?

Accepting Christ means transferring your trust from whatever you once trusted in to now trusting God. Accepting Christ means making Him Lord and Master of your life. "Thy will be done." What does that imply? When we pray "Thy will be done," total surrender should take place. Our wills are abandoned as we ask Christ to work in us, letting Him change whatever He sees that needs fixing. A releasing of our faith takes place. We will not become robots. We will still have choices to make, but we will no longer "lean on our own understanding" (Proverbs 3:5-6). At the time when we release our will, we actually become winners. We win the bliss of knowing that Jesus is truly ours. We win peace of mind (Isaiah 26:3). We win unspeakable joy (1 Peter 1:8). Worry and doubt are tools that Satan uses to distract us. If

he can get our minds on a problem instead of remembering the problem solver, chances are that we will become afraid. Instead of looking up, we will become down trodden. We become weak and fragile. We might even try to make things better ourselves. Releasing our will to God will rid us of the situation.

Another tool that Satan likes to use is pride. A number of people often brag about their accomplishments without ever acknowledging the source. Some even take pride stating that they are a self- made person. For those persons, seeking God's will for their lives doesn't seem to be of any value. For some with that way of thinking, reality sets in and they realize the error of such thoughts. The Bible points out time and time again instances when God's children fail to surrender their will to God.

We, as Christians, should always acknowledge the source of our blessings. We know that our help comes from the Lord. Surrendering our will to God is the only way to truly experience all He has in store for us. Daily, we must pray for the depths of our hearts. "Thy will" be done. Turn your will over to God and win.

GOD SPEAKS...
W.O.W (SURRENDER)
WINNING OVER WILL

ISAIAH 12:2

Behold, God is my salvation; I will trust, and not be afraid: for the LORD JEHOVAH is my strength and my song; he also is become my salvation.

PSALM 9:10

And they that know thy name will put their trust in thee: for thou, LORD, hast not forsaken them that seek thee.

PSALM 37:23

The steps of a good man are ordered by the LORD: and he delighteth in his way.

PROVERBS 3:5-6

Trust in the LORD with all thine heart; and lean not unto thine own understanding. In all thy ways acknowledge him, and he shall direct thy paths.

ROMANS 12:2

And be not conformed to this world: but be ye transformed by the renewing of your mind, that ye may prove what is that good, and acceptable, and perfect, will of God.

Hebrews 10:36

For ye have need of patience, that, after ye have done the will of God, ye might receive the promise.

Philippians 2:13

For it is God which worketh in you both to will and to do of his good pleasure.

1 Thessalonians 5:18

In everything give thanks: for this is the will of God in Christ Jesus concerning you.

1 Peter 4:19

Wherefore let them that suffer according to the will of God commit the keeping of their souls to him in well doing, as unto a faithful Creator.

Micah 6:8

He hath shewed thee, O man, what is good; and what doth the LORD require of thee, but to do justly, and to love mercy, and to walk humbly with thy God?

Luke 9:23-24 (NASB)

And He was saying to them all, "If anyone wishes to come after Me, he must deny himself, and take up his cross daily and follow Me. For whoever wishes to save his life will lose it, but whoever loses his life for My sake, he is the one who will save it.

ROMANS 14:8

For whether we live, we live unto the Lord; and whether we die, we die unto the Lord: whether we live therefore, or die, we are the Lord's.

COLOSSIANS 2:6-7

As ye have therefore received Christ Jesus the Lord, so walk ye in him. Rooted and built up in him, and stablished in the faith, as ye have been taught, abounding therein with thanksgiving.

JOSHUA 24:24(MSG)

The people answered Joshua, "We will worship God. What he says, we'll do."

BLESSED ASSURANCES

Select a scripture from the *God Speaks* section to reflect on each day. Write the scripture in the space provided. After reading and meditating on the scripture during the day, take time to write down the assurance from our Father you received from the passage.

DAY1 _____

_____

_____

_____

DAY2 _____

_____

_____

_____

DAY3 _____

_____

_____

_____

DAY4 _____

_____

_____

_____

DAY5_____

_____

_____

_____

DAY6_____

_____

_____

_____

DAY7_____

_____

_____

_____

THE TRUTH

Write out the truths that you gained during the week.

THANKSGIVINGS

Write a prayer of thanksgiving to God for what He is doing in your life.

ALL THINGS NEW
LIVING IN THE NOW

Dear Daughters,

Yesterday is gone; tomorrow has not arrived. The present is here waiting to be enjoyed. Each day is a new gift from our heavenly Father. It's a new opportunity to enjoy God's wonderful blessings. What stands in the way of our enjoying the gift of a new day God has to offer? Worry, doubt, fear, anxiety are often hindrances to the enjoyment of God's blessings.

When we are able to put the past behind us and stop worrying about what will happen in the future, we are able to look at each day as a new beginning. David stated in Psalm118:24, "This is a day the Lord has made we will rejoice and be glad in it." All things are truly new; it's your mindset that might be old. In Psalm 51:10 David asked God to create in him a clean heart and renew the right spirit within him. This request should be part of our prayer each morning. New opportunities are available to experience the faithfulness of God. We have new opportunities to realize just how awesome God truly is. Don't listen to the lies of the devil. Satan is trying to keep you downtrodden. The devil specializes in trying to destroy hope. Don't fall for his tricks. When we surrender ourselves to God all things can truly be new (Corinthians 5:17). God's supply of blessings will

never run out. Learning to trust God fully is the best way to appreciate our relationship with Him. Once we surrender our will to Him, we can rest on His promises. God's Word is full of assurances of His love for us. As we study and meditate on the Word of God, we become renewed. We are able daily to see His faithfulness as we spend time remembering the center of our joy. In Jeremiah 15:15-16 we find these words:

"O Lord, Thou knowest: remember me, and visit me, and revenge me of my persecutors; take me not away in Thy longsuffering: know that for Thy sake I have suffered rebuke. Thy Words were found, and I did eat them; and Thy Word was unto me the joy and rejoicing of mine heart: for I am called by Thy Name, O Lord God of hosts."

In order for us to experience joy that surpasses all understanding, we must stay in the presence of God. Each day before our feet hit the floor we need to thank God for another day and invite Him to lead the way. Keeping our mind focused on God allows us to develop an attitude of gratitude. The focus will not be on what we do not have but on what we do have. We have a Savior that loves us unconditionally. We have a God that neither slumbers nor sleeps, a strong tower, a rock, a fortress, and I am sure we could add volumes more to the list, but I think you get the point. God is an awesome God who is truly the center of our joy. Let's turn our attention to what Paul stated in Philippians 3:12-14 *"Not that I have already obtained it or have already become perfect,*

but I press on so that I may lay hold of that for which also I was laid hold of by Christ Jesus. Brethren, I do not regard myself as having laid hold of it yet; but one thing I do: forgetting what lies behind and reaching forward to what lies ahead, I press on toward the goal for the prize of the upward call of God in Christ Jesus" (NASB) .
Today and every day press toward the mark remembering with God all things are new.

GOD SPEAKS...
ALL THINGS NEW
(LIVING IN THE NOW)

LAMENTATIONS 3:22-24 (NASB)

The unfailing love of the LORD never ends! By his mercies we have been kept from complete destruction. Great is his faithfulness; his mercies begin afresh each day. I say to myself, "The LORD is my inheritance; therefore, I will hope in him!"

EZEKIEL 36:25-27 (NLT)

"Then I will sprinkle clean water on you, and you will be clean. Your filth will be washed away, and you will no longer worship idols. And I will give you a new heart with new and right desires, and I will put a new spirit in you. I will take out your stony heart of sin and give you a new, obedient heart. And I will put my Spirit in you so you will obey my laws and do whatever I command."

PHILIPPIANS 3:13-14 (NLT)

No, dear brothers and sisters, I am still not all I should be, but I am focusing all my energies on this one thing: Forgetting the past and looking forward to what lies ahead, I strain to reach the end of the race and receive the prize for which God, through Christ Jesus, is calling us up to heaven.

HEBREWS 12:10-11

Our fathers disciplined us for a little while as they thought best; but God disciplines us for our good, that we may share in his holiness. No discipline seems pleasant at the time, but painful. Later on, however, it produces a harvest of righteousness and peace for those who have been.

ISAIAH 54:10

For the mountains shall depart, and the hills be removed; but my kindness shall not depart from thee, neither shall the covenant of my peace be removed, saith the LORD that hath mercy on thee.

PROVERBS 12:25

Heaviness in the heart of man maketh it stoop: but a good word maketh it glad.righteousness and peace for those who have been.

ROMANS 8:37

Nay, in all these things we are more than conquerors through him that loved us.

2 CORINTHIANS 5:17

Therefore if any man be in Christ, he is a new creature: old things are passed away; behold, all things are become new.

HEBREWS 13:6

So that we may boldly say, The Lord is my helper, and I will not fear what man shall do unto me.

1 Peter 5:7

Casting all your care upon him; for he careth for you.

John 1:12

But as many as received him, to them gave he power to become the sons of God, even to them that believe on his name.

Romans 8:15

For ye have not receivedt he spirit of bondage again to fear; but ye have received the Spirit of adoption, whereby we cry, Abba, Father.

Ephesians 2:19

Now therefore ye are no more strangers and foreigners, but fellow citizens with the saints, and of the household of God.

1 Peter 1:3-5

Blessed be the God and Father of our Lord Jesus Christ, which according to his abundant mercy hath begotten us again unto a lively hope by the resurrection of Jesus Christ from the dead.

BLESSED ASSURANCES

Select a scripture from the *God Speaks* section to reflect on each day. Write the scripture in the space provided. After reading and meditating on the scripture during the day, take time to write down the assurance from our Father you received from the passage.

DAY1_____

_____

_____

_____

DAY2_____

_____

_____

_____

DAY3_____

_____

_____

_____

DAY4_____

_____

_____

_____

DAY5 _____

_____

_____

_____

DAY6 _____

_____

_____

_____

DAY7 _____

_____

_____

_____

THE TRUTH

Write out the truths that you gained during the week.

THANKSGIVINGS

Write a prayer of thanksgiving to God for what He is
doing in your life.

ABOUT THE AUTHOR

Bonita Williams, a vessel of God, resides in Atlanta, GA with her husband, Benny. She is the blessed mother of two phenomenal daughters, Benecia and Breyuna. She has two awesome grandchildren, Amber and Ishmael. Her strongest desire is to be used by God in any way He sees fit.

FOR ADDITIONAL COPIES OF THIS BOOK PLEASE CONTACT:

Vision Inspired Publications
P.O. Box 44486
Atlanta, GA 30336

visioninspiredpublications25@gmail.com
www.inspireddivinely.com